Her

Kritisha Amatya

BookLeaf Publishing

India | USA | UK

Her © 2024 Kritisha Amatya

All rights reserved.

No part of this publication may be reproduced, stored in a retrieval system, or transmitted, in any form or by any means, electronic, mechanical, photocopying, recording or otherwise, without the prior written permission of the presenters.

Kritisha Amatya asserts the moral right to be identified as author of this work.

Presentation by *BookLeaf Publishing*

Web: www.bookleafpub.com

E-mail: info@bookleafpub.com

ISBN: 9789363314085

First edition 2024

To the ones who believed I could and the one
who inspired me<3

ACKNOWLEDGEMENT

I would like to thank everyone who helped me participate in this challenge, Ubin Malla, my mama, and Tejita Vaidya Amatya, my mother. I would also like to thank Urvi Agrawal, my friend and didi who presented me with this opportunity and someone who believed in my writing since the sixth grade.

Dream Girl

I had dreamt of a girl who was a little like me
She'd smile big at the world ignoring its cruelty
I had dreamt of a girl who loved poetry
Someone who spoke in whimsical rhymes
fluently

So when I saw her sitting in my seat
My heart joyfully skipped a beat
"Thank you god" I whispered as I neared her
I sat down, the world effectively starting to blur

The girl from my dream was sitting beside me
With long caramel hair and a pile of books, I
mean who else could it be?
My mouth moved of its own accord completely
unplanned
The thoughts in my head not even I could
understand

I uttered the words "Are you a poet?"
She looked at me like I was trying to uncover
her secret
God, how embarrassing! What had I just done
But she smiled and she replied, "No, not really
just trying to become one."

I smiled back unaware of what to say
"I'm in love with you! Be mine!" I think and turn
away
And as if she'd read my mind she slips me a note
which says,
"Though I'm not a poet, would you get coffee
with me anyways?"

Sweet Conversations

Coffee dates aren't my thing
The awkward "Hellos" only lead to meaningless
flings
But I arrived to the spot early anyway
Hoping against hope this date would go my way

I got her white flowers
Daisies with lavender towers
"I hope she isn't allergic to anything" I say out
loud
"She isn't don't worry" a voice answered from
within the crowd

There she was, a bouquet in hand
"Wanted to get you something" she says
brushing away a strand
Her shy smile is light and gentle
And the thought of this moment makes me just a
little sentimental

As both of us stand there unsure of what to do
I could hear the gods whisper, "Just kiss you
two!"
The thought makes me giggle and I take a step
forward
I take her hand in mine trying not to be awkward

We walk to the cafe in comfortable silence
Taking in each other's aura in the short distance
I hand her the flowers as we sit down
Hoping she would like them and do anything but
frown

She smiles even brighter
And my heart gives a flutter
Sure that the gods had written about us in the
constellations
Our date goes perfectly with coffee and sweet
conversations

The Giver

She is like a rose growing amidst a bush of
thorns
Her beauty so radiant you could feel it in your
bones
Like someone you would call an angel god sent
Knowing time with her was time well spent

Her eyes are lakes of honey dew
And like her smile she views the world gently
too
She is what I would call a 'giver'
Someone who will give and give even when
their hands start to blister

I worry she will soon lose her mind
For the world is too cruel and she, too kind
And I know I asked for someone like me
But I am not a person you should aspire to be

Yet she helps others with a kind embrace
Saying that "Everyone deserves your grace."
It is not fair that she sees the good in everyone
When no one seems to return her warmth, not
even some

She is the person everyone turns to
Someone willing to wipe away your tears and sit
with you
Her presence itself is like being showered in
sunlight
Like with her by your side you can win any fight

Even though she knows that helping others
won't heal her
She holds her head high and keeps her heart pure
She will say what she believes in without a
doubt or fear
And all I can say is that I'm falling in love with
her

Be Mine

Words scare me
Words are like cages that will never set you free
It seems like a joke considering I'm a writer
But the words that are trapped in me seem to
squeeze my throat tighter

"Just ask her out" a voice in me whispers
Even the slight thought of rejection holds me
back in my endeavours
"If she says no I will never see her again" I
counter my brain
"Why would she say no" my brain fires back
again

I am too scared to let this bittersweet part go
The part where we are friends or a little more, I
don't know
I want to see her everyday and call her every
night
If that means we stay friends that would be
alright

But she wanted more that I could tell
So she sat me down looking nervous as hell
Slowly but surely taking my smile as a sign
She muttered the phrase, "Will you be mine?"

Strawberry Kisses

She tastes like strawberries
Like a warm hug in the autumn breeze
She smells like cinnamon
Like rolls engulfed in glaze and made with
compassion

She feels like soft dove feathers
Like a blanket wrapped around your shoulders
She sounds like sweet songs of the stars
Like the song that could heal all of your scars

She looks like heaven trapped in a human being
Like one glance could wipe away the misery
you've seen
She looks greater than the greatest sunsets
Like a whisper of freedom from all your sins and
all your debts

She is like being showered in stardust
A blessing from the universe that words do not
just
Like the moon itself left fragments in her soul
And I suspected the sun itself granted her a
coronal

I knew for sure however
That she would be a mortal goddess amongst us
forever
With her ethereal beauty and unwavering love
Her strength and passion all something to be in
awe of

She is peace and faith
My peace, my faith, and deserving of eternal
grace
My flower, my love, my queen
I would stay by her side even if it meant grief
even if it meant travelling worlds unseen

Moonlit Dances

Dancing is my favourite thing
Heart to heart and skin to skin
So when we stopped in the middle of our walk
To sit down under the moon and talk

I pulled out my phone and picked out a song
Without even thinking she began to sing along
I held out my hand
We got up swaying gently to our favourite band

The scene felt surreal
Hoping that this time, this time she'd be the one
life can't steal
The wind in our hair and moon light on our skin
For a moment it felt like god had forgiven all we
had sinned

In the brief moments where we remained in
rhythm
I could see a life, happy in our own little
kingdom
I would grant her the world if she ever so
wondered
I would lay the stars at her feet if she ever
desired

I would give up all magic for this girl
For she was a gift life itself had given me, a
goddess matched with a feeble mortal
She was worth all moments of despair
All cries and pleads that rattled my bones, all
torments I had deemed unfair

Under the moon, in the minutes where all
seemed wonderful
In a dream which felt far from real
She was mine and I was hers
With our moonlit dances and blissful tears

Flower Crowns

In a garden far away from the cities
In a world of our own where we could breathe
with ease
The world stopped just for a moment
The trees whispered tales of the old and the sun
remained in the sky; persistent

We sat amongst a ornate array of flowers
Each one greeting this new chapter of ours
White clovers danced between her fingers and
her gown
As she wove them gently into an elegant crown

She placed the crown slowly on my head
And she smiled gazing at her work but I was
gazing at her instead
The crown belonged to her by right
For being brave and showing might

She grew more lovely each day
And I grew short of words to say
How much she meant to me
How much I willed the universe to agree

Like summer days and flower crowns
And soft silk and home made gowns
Eternal faith for eternal believers
Her and I were meant to be one anothers

What if

The shadows dance as I lie awake
One gruesome thought that I couldn't quite
shake
What if this was just another heartbreak waiting
to happen?
What if I was just mistaken?

My heart whispered a silent prayer
Willing the universe to be just and fair
But what if this was just another test
Another lesson to suggest that being lonely was
being blessed

Was being happy just for a moment
Worth the loneliness and upcoming torment?
Was I willing to trust the gods once again?
Did I ever have a choice to begin?

Unconditional

15

The chains placed around love's neck is a simple
thing called condition
Condition shapes the love you get and give by
definition
That has been love's limitations since forever
Like a false promise of freedom on the lips of a
worker

Love should not be bound by shackles
Should not be tied down by manacles
Love should be free and without bounds
Given and received without any grounds

Need

In the nights that I can not see
Can not feel and can not be
I cry into the moon's loving arms
Wiping my tears with her gentle palms

The darkness seems to consume me everytime
Drowning me in my worries, thoughts that had
no song, no rhyme
I begged each night for a hand to pull me out
Pleading to the endless sky that someone would
hear me shout

As my screams grew louder and my hope grew
weaker
I gave up on the thought of my saviour
That is when she grasped my hand
Pulled me up, brushed off the dust and helped
me stand

She pulled me in her warm embrace
Wiping all the tears from my face
She sat with me until I grew tired
Of the telling and retelling of my time as a child

She gave me pieces of broken stars
Helped me fit them into my scars
She told me I deserved everything good the
universe has to offer
And I replied all I needed was her

Falling from the skies

The wind whispered in my ears
A nudge to tell the tales of my fears
To tell her the truth of who I am
Why I am

I am scared of many things
Like a windchime of worries hung on thin
strings
"I am afraid" is the first thing I tell her
She does nothing but move closer

"Afraid of what?" She presses forward
And I told her why I thought I was a coward
I let my darkness seep from my being
The cold hatred I was used to feeling

I told her of the red that lined my body
Of the sheets that still lay bloody
I told her of the monster in my head
The one they called depression instead

She took my hand and gazed into my eyes
Her eyes peered deep into my soul uncovering
my truths and all my lies
I waited for her to turn away
"I understand if this is too much" I say

Expecting her to shy from the shattered pieces
that now lay in front of her
"You are amazing" she said, barely a whisper
Tears now lining her honey dew eyes
Falling with the weight of falling from the skies

Our fictional life

I can not say we did not fight
In the year that passed, we were quite a sight
In moments some we drifted apart
Then came back to each other with a heavy heart

We became best friends
Denying any unruly ends
I would like to say we became eternal
Something I thought was only fictional

But as the days passed in a blur
I stopped remembering life before her
Life right now was all I craved
Life right now was life well made

And even as we built our lives
Me writing books and her saving lives
We came home to each other
After a long day of words and disorder

We sat side by side watching our favourite show
Finally the world moving slow
We take in this little life we built
Happy and grateful with no regret no guilt

Until you die

You only live until you die
So live all you want or at least try
But when you do try and believe life is on your
side
Everything comes crashing down like a
landslide

Her scent grew fainter and books collected dust
Her clothes lay in a box in my attic and her hair
pins collected rust
I saw her only after hours in the small grave
where she lay
Once again someone I love was sadly taken
away

She died in my arms in the cramped up hospital
room
In her stained hospital gown and patiently
awaiting her doom
She took a piece of my heart with her
To heavens above her new home forever

My days grew darker
As she grew sicker
And when the grim reaper cam to greet her

I was still clutching her hand my words
beginning to slur

She told me to live life on her behalf
She told me to party at her funeral, forcing a
laugh
I however could not return her smile
I was still in deep denial

How could it be that the one person so important
to me
Could be ripped away so easily
How could my heart go on without this person
Someone who had become my life's best
fraction

Empty

Do not trust the gods
Do not try to defy the odds
Life will quite literally slap you in the face
Never believe when someone tells you the gods
will show you grace

Life does not work on a system of merit
It serves as a horrible experience when you least
expect it
Like an endless cycle of jokes you can't quite
escape
Giving and snatching people you can't quite
replace

I became angry that night
I stormed outside looking for a fight
When I found none I turned to the sky
I screamed at the gods until all I could do was
cry

I woke up in the street the following morning
The clouds loomed above and the wind howled
in grief as if they too were in mourning
The walk home passed in a fast paced blur

The world seemed so unaffected about losing
her

Only I seemed to be left screaming
Trying to pick up the pieces only to be left
bleeding
Life drained out of me as her breath had done
Only emptiness filled the void where love had
once begun

Broken Pictures

Photographs are stolen times
Like hearts composed in song and rhymes
My rhymes had stopped my songs had paused
Nothing could wake me from the pain her loss
had caused

I lay there in a pile of broken memories
Replaying the most loving of stories
Deep within me, a voice told me she'd want me
to be happy
But all I could do was damn the gods for doing
this to me

After all, what had I done?
Fallen in love with a hope that had none?
Or was it that I had begun to care?
For someone more than was allowed my share?

Why I was punished I did not understand
For dreaming of an impossible wonderland?
Perhaps it was my flaw to trust
The gods when reprimand was must

Perhaps I am destined an eternity
Maybe broken hearts is my destiny

Perhaps the gods gift only dim flickers
Of merriment which fills broken pictures

Once was

27

I often think of what once was
Of what it became or what was the cause
Death can not be undone
Can not be shielded can not be overcome

So I pretend I pretend I am ok
I pretend, though I'm sick of it, I pretend I am
not slipping away
I pretend to be listening
I pretend to be understanding

I pretend she is still here
I pretend she will always stay near
I pretend she is not a universe away
I pretend she will always stay

I pretend it is what once it was
And imagine life is not yet a lost cause
Even without her
Even if love for someone alive would never
again stir

Shattered Pieces

 I woke up one day and decided I could not write
anymore of heartbreak
For my heart broke away bit by bit everyday for
her sake
Every shattered piece fell from my heart
I didn't know where to end or where to start

How do you measure the magnitude of hurt?
How can one overcome its gurt?
Was it as impossible as it felt?
Or was it just me with a terrible hand of cards
dealt?

How would I pick up my shattered self
Would I even have the strength to accept what I
felt
Shattered pieces don't belong
No matter how much you plead or how long

To the Gods

I think the time is running out
I think I have no more energy to shout
I think I have stopped breathing around you
I think that the fact you did this for me was
never true

For the fear of arrows sent down my throat
For the fear of drowning in her blood instead of
float
I think it has finally come to the point where the
dagger pushed into my heart summons no pain
Adds no more gain

I looked you straight in the eyes as you berated
me for making mistakes you made up
Claimed you gave me hope
And I felt nothing but cold. Dead. Hatred.
I think the time is running out and I am ready to
leave. This beautiful lie she and I created

www.ingramcontent.com/pod-product-compliance
Lightning Source LLC
LaVergne TN
LVHW041252200726
843507LV00013B/2924